STEM CAREERS

Health Care Careers

Christine Wilcox

ReferencePoint Press®

San Diego, CA

ReferencePoint Press®

About the Author

Christine Wilcox writes fiction and nonfiction for young adults and adults. She has worked as an editor, an instructional designer, and a writing instructor. She lives in Richmond, Virginia, with her husband, David, and her son, Anthony.

For more information, contact:
ReferencePoint Press, Inc.
PO Box 27779
San Diego, CA 92198
www.ReferencePointPress.com

Picture Credits:

Cover: Steve Debenport/iStockphoto.com
6: Maury Aaseng
21: Monkey Business Images/Shutterstock.com
29: Christopher Penler/Shutterstock.com
43: Antonio Guillem/Shutterstock.com
50: Moodbaord/Thinkstock Images
67: Dmytro Zinkevych/Shutterstock.com

LIBRARY OF CONGRESS CATALOGING-IN-PUBLICATION DATA

Name: Wilcox, Christine, author.
Title: Health Care Careers/by Christine Wilcox.
Description: San Diego, CA: ReferencePoint Press, Inc., 2019. | Series: STEM Careers | Audience: Grades 9 to 12. | Includes bibliographical references and index.
Identifiers: LCCN 2017054321 (print) | LCCN 2017060825 (ebook) | ISBN 9781682824344 (eBook) | ISBN 9781682824337 (hardback)
Subjects: LCSH: Medicine—Vocational guidance—Juvenile literature. | Medical personnel—Juvenile literature. | Allied health personnel—Vocational guidance—Juvenile literature.
Classification: LCC R690 (ebook) | LCC R690 .W5425 2019 (print) | DDC 610.69—dc23

Contents

Health Care: The Fastest-Growing Industry

The Garfield Innovation Center in San Leandro, California, has an operating room, an emergency department, and a birthing room. But there are no patients at Garfield—instead, medical professionals use the center to improve their skills and test innovative procedures. In May 2017 more than three hundred high school students filled the center during Garfield's Youth Career Day. They performed mock surgeries, watched a birth with a simulation dummy, practiced positive bedside manner, and tracked a hypothetical teenager who was being treated for depression. "Students can envision themselves in actual settings that represents where health care is going," explained Nikki West, co-organizer of the event. As she told Anna Fiddler in a May 2017 article posted on Kaiser Permanente's website, Look InsideKP Northern California, "It also encourages young people to expand their notion of future fields of study."

Not Just Doctors and Nurses

One of the goals of Garfield's Career Day and similar programs across the country is to make young people aware that becoming a doctor or nurse is not the only way to have a career in health care. It is true that doctors (who diagnose and treat disease) and nurses (who care for patients and in most cases administer the treatments that doctors have prescribed) make up the core of the

4

health care system. But there are hundreds of other professionals involved in patient care. As a group, these people are known as allied health care professionals. Some assist doctors (medical assistants and surgical technologists), some help fill prescriptions (pharmacy technicians and opticians), and some help people eat right (nutritionists) or recover from injuries (physical therapists). One especially large and varied field within allied health care is medical technology. Medical technicians and technologists receive highly specialized training that allows them to do testing and laboratory work. Some, like phlebotomists (the technicians who draw blood from patients) train for only a year after high school. Others, like diagnostic medical sonographers, go to college for two to four years to learn how to operate complex ultrasound equipment and interpret test results.

Some allied health care jobs, such as home health aide, pay only slightly more than minimum wage, but many other jobs offer excellent salaries. For instance, the Bureau of Labor Statistics (BLS) reports that certified occupational therapy assistants (COTAs) make a median salary of $56,950 per year. These professionals help patients develop or recover skills they need to perform daily tasks. The BLS projects that COTA jobs will grow by 43 percent by 2024, which means that COTAs will be in high demand in the future.

In addition to allied health care careers, there are a growing number of administrative jobs available in health care. One such job is medical coder, administrative professionals who assign codes to health care diagnoses and procedures to make sure the provider receives all appropriate compensation from the insurance company for services rendered to the patient. The average salary of a medical coder is now almost $50,000, and at least ten thousand coding jobs were created in 2016. "The coding profession is a great opportunity for individuals seeking their first job, and it's attractive to a lot of medical professionals burned out on patient care," said Raemarie Jimenez, a vice president at the American Academy of Professional Coders. As she told Chad Terhune in an April 2017 article in the *New York Times*, "There is a lot of opportunity once you've got a foot in the door."

Careers in Health Care

Occupation	Minimal Educational Requirement	2016 Median Pay
Chiropractor	Doctoral or professional degree	$67,520
Dentist	Doctoral or professional degree	$159,770
Dietitian and nutritionist	Bachelor's degree	$58,920
EMT and paramedic	Postsecondary non-degree award	$32,670
Home health aide and personal care aide	High school diploma or equivalent	$22,170
Medical records and health information technician	Postsecondary non-degree award	$38,040
Pharmacist	Doctoral or professional degree	$122,230
Pharmacy technician	High school diploma or equivalent	$30,920
Physical therapist	Doctoral or professional degree	$85,400
Registered nurse	Bachelor's degree	$68,450
Speech-language pathologist	Master's degree	$74,680

Source: Bureau of Labor Statistics, *Occupational Outlook Handbook.* www.bls.gov.

A Satisfying Career with a Bright Future

Health care is an attractive career choice for today's young people for several reasons. Overall job growth in this sector has increased dramatically in recent years and shows no sign of stopping. The population in the United States is getting older, and advances in health care mean that people are living longer than ever before. This means that the demand for health care will only increase in the coming decades. That demand was also bolstered by health insurance reform, which has given millions of people access to health care—some for the first time. Because of these factors, many experts assert that the health care industry is on track to be the single largest job sector in the United States. In fact, the BLS predicts that by 2022, the health care industry will support over 21 million jobs. In 2017 about 4.5 million of those jobs paid a middle-class wage, a number that is projected to increase.

Careers in health care also offer a great deal of job satisfaction. Most people enter this field because they have a desire to help others. Some enjoy providing direct patient care, while some prefer to work behind the scenes. But overall, most health care professionals feel that helping people is consistently rewarding and adds to their overall job satisfaction. In fact, these jobs regularly rank as the most satisfying and meaningful of all professions. In an April 2017 article on the website Verywell, medical recruiter Andrea Santiago had this to say about choosing a career in health care: "You could help bring a new life into the world or save a life from ending. You can change lives, impacting families the way only healthcare professionals are able to."

Psychologist

Psychologists are scientists who study the human mind. They tend to be intensely curious about the thought processes and experiences of other people. "I love to hear people's stories: who they are, why they are, and how they got to the who and the why," explained psychologist Ildiko Tabori in a February 2016 interview published on the website ValuePenguin. Tabori is a psychologist who specializes in helping comedians deal with the stresses of their profession. She works at the world-famous comedy club the Laugh Factory in Los Angeles, California. "I think the lifestyle of a standup comedian can breed more of a depressive life," she explained. "They're out on the road, they're sad, they are away from family and friends, and they don't have their support systems right next to them." In addition to her successful private practice in Los Angeles, Tabori watches comedians perform their sets and helps them deal with everything from loneliness to suicidal urges. Her career is an example of how varied the work of a psychologist can be. "Every day is different," she said. "I do more than just therapy.

At a Glance

Psychologist

Minimum Educational Requirements
Doctoral degree, although some specialties only require a master's degree

Personal Qualities
Strong analytical skills, empathy, curiosity, excellent listening skills

Certification and Licensing
Required in most states

Working Conditions
Indoors in an office or clinical setting

Salary Range
About $40,000 to $150,000

Number of Jobs
About 173,900

Future Job Outlook
Much faster than average

There are days when I do psychological testing and . . . other days when I work on forensic and other types of clinical evaluations. . . . I have yet to have one day be exactly like another day."

When people are seeking help with an emotional problem or a mental health issue, they are likely to see a clinical psychologist like Tabori—a nonmedical doctor who specializes in treating mental health disorders. However, there are dozens of different types of psychologists and dozens more specialties within those types. For instance, developmental psychologists specialize in the brain's development over the human life span, school psychologists help children succeed in an academic setting, forensic psychologists specialize in how the law treats psychological issues and sometimes act as expert witnesses in trials, and neuropsychologists diagnose and treat brain-based disorders like Alzheimer's disease or autism spectrum disorder. And some psychologists do not specialize in mental disorders at all. For example, occupational psychologists study the psychology of the workplace, and psychologists who specialize in positive psychology study happiness and fulfillment.

Some psychologists enjoy variety and choose to treat a wide range of disorders. Others choose to focus on their specific interests. For example, a psychologist interested in the effects of trauma might specialize in treating children who undergo trauma or abuse; soldiers who suffer from post-traumatic stress disorder; or victims of disaster, domestic violence, or violent crimes. Or he or she might focus on researching the effects of trauma or the effectiveness of various treatments.

Psychologists are also trained to administer tests, a process known as psychological assessment. Psychologists usually arrive at their diagnoses with the help of standardized tests. These tests can take many forms. Sometimes the psychologist will ask the patient a series of questions designed to reveal aspects of a person's psychology; other times the patient will be given tasks to complete while under observation. Psychologists are trained to administer these tests correctly and to interpret the results. Psychologists interested in assessment can also specialize in developing new psychological tests.

Even though psychologists diagnose and treat mental health disorders, they are not medical doctors, and therefore they are not permitted to prescribe medication. For this reason, many psychologists work in partnership with psychiatrists—medical doctors who specialize in mental disorders and the various drugs that treat them.

How Do You Become a Psychologist?

Education

Nearly all types of psychologists must have a doctoral degree in psychology to be able to legally use the title "psychologist" or to offer psychological services to patients. (Exceptions include occupational psychologists and some types of school psychologists.) According to surveys conducted by the American Psychological Association (APA), a doctoral degree in psychology takes about seven years, on average, of additional schooling after earning a bachelor's degree. Two types of degrees are available: a doctor of psychology (PsyD), which emphasizes practical work with patients, and a PhD in psychology, which emphasizes research.

Earning a doctoral degree is extremely challenging. It usually entails writing a dissertation—a long research paper of publishable quality. Dissertations can be hundreds of pages long and take years to write. Doctoral programs also require students to take classes, teach or do research, and work with patients under the supervision of a psychologist. It is an arduous process that is not for everyone. "When you're ready to go to grad school, really truly think it through, because this is a huge commitment in your life," advised Tabori. "Your life is being held in somebody else's hands for quite a while."

Students who are mainly interested in treating patients sometimes opt to earn a master's degree in psychology and become licensed therapists instead of psychologists. These programs take about two years to complete.

10

Certification and Licensing

Almost all states require psychologists to be licensed. In general, licensing requires that a person hold a PsyD or a PhD in psychology, complete an internship, and pass an exam. These requirements vary depending on the specialty. For example, according to the National Association of School Psychologists, most states require that school psychologists have at least a master's degree with sixty or more credits in school psychology, complete a twelve-hundred-hour internship, and pass a licensing exam. Licenses are specialty specific; for instance, a school psychologist may not practice other forms of psychology. These strict rules are designed to protect both the public and the integrity of the profession. Licenses must be renewed periodically, and renewal usually requires completion of continuing education courses.

Volunteer Work and Internships

Psychologists must complete formal internships in order to be licensed. However, college and even high school students can gain experience in therapeutic techniques by volunteering to take calls at crisis hotlines. These volunteers receive training to be able to provide support for people who may not have a friend or family member in whom they can confide. They are also trained to be able to identify situations where a caller may be in danger of self-harm or may be suffering from a mental disorder. There are also volunteer opportunities in mental health clinics, crisis centers, and hospitals. These facilities need caring, discreet volunteers to staff their reception areas and assist medical professionals with patient care.

Skills and Personality

The best psychologists are intensely curious about how the human mind works. They are genuinely interested in listening to other people's problems and in helping them better understand themselves. This takes patience and empathy, as well as strong listening and observational skills. Psychologists also have to have strong analytical and problem-solving skills to be able to diagnose patients and help them with treatment plans.

Employers

About one in three psychologists are self-employed. Many of these are clinical psychologists in private practice, either working alone or as part of a practice group. Clinical psychologists also work in health care facilities, such as hospitals, mental health clinics, or rehabilitation centers. School psychologists work in public and private schools. Industrial-organizational psychologists work in human resources departments, federal or state agencies, or consulting firms. Psychologists who do research may work independently or be employed by universities, government agencies, or private research organizations. Psychologists also teach at colleges and universities.

Working Conditions

Psychologists usually work in an office setting, and most create a comfortable space to treat patients. Some psychologists work in hospitals or clinics. Psychologists in private practice set their own hours, while those who work in health care facilities usually work regular business hours.

Earnings

According to the Bureau of Labor Statistics (BLS), in May 2016 the median salary for a psychologist was $75,230, with the lowest-paid 10 percent earning about $41,900 and the highest-paid 10 percent earning about $121,600 per year. Clinical psychologists in private practice or who are employed in outpatient care centers (medical centers that specialize in care that does not require an overnight stay) can earn substantially more. The BLS notes that the average salary of psychologists who work in outpatient care is $142,780, and the website Best Psychology Degrees estimates that those in private practice can potentially earn $150,000 or more.

Opportunities for Advancement

Psychologists can advance their careers by specializing in an aspect of psychology and increasing their expertise in that area. For instance, as the population ages, there will be a need for more psychologists with expertise in psychological issues related to aging. Psychologists who work in health care settings can move into supervision or administration positions. Psychologists who do research can advance their careers by publishing in academic journals.

What Is the Future Outlook for Psychologists?

The BLS projects that employment prospects for psychologists will grow by 19 percent from 2014 to 2024, a much faster rate than average. The highest demand will be in the fields of clinical, counseling, and school psychology. Industrial-organizational psychologists will also see substantial growth, but because this is a small field, the BLS projects only about four hundred new jobs will be added during the ten-year period.

One reason for the increase is that the stigma against seeking mental health treatment is waning. More and more people are seeking treatment for mental illness or for help dealing with the challenges of life. At the same time, the population is aging. Older people face unique mental health challenges, including depression, dementia, and degenerative brain diseases, such as Alzheimer's disease. Geropsychologists—psychologists who specialize in mental disorders of aging—will become more in demand, as will clinical and counseling psychologists who treat older adults.

Another reason for the growth in this field is that people are becoming more aware of the connection between mental health and learning. More school psychologists will be needed to help students with special needs, learning disabilities, and issues such as bullying or drug or alcohol use. In addition, advances in the diagnosis and treatment of brain-based disorders such as attention-deficit/hyperactivity disorder and autism spectrum disorder have increased the need for neuropsychologists and clinical psychologists specializing in these issues.

Even with rapid growth in this field, the APA warns that psychologists who have only master's degrees will find it more and more difficult to practice, as many states require a doctoral degree for licensing, and most organizations prefer to hire doctoral-level practitioners. In addition, psychologists who offer only talk therapy (as opposed to those who offer other services such as testing) will see increased competition from licensed therapists and counselors who charge less for their services. To remain competitive, psychologists interested in talk therapy should specialize in areas that interest them.

Even with these challenges, the future for psychologists with strong credentials and special expertise is bright. Students pursuing this field can look forward to a fascinating and fulfilling career with excellent earning potential.

Find Out More

American Psychological Association (APA)
750 First St. NE
Washington, DC 20002
website: www.apa.org

The APA is the largest professional organization of psychologists in the United States. Its website has information about all aspects of psychology, from the science of psychology to information about mental illness. It also has detailed information for students and teachers about pursuing a career as a psychologist.

Careers in Psychology
website: http://careersinpsychology.org

Careers in Psychology is a website dedicated to helping students interested in this career. The website includes a detailed description of hundreds of job titles related to psychology, information about academic programs and their requirements, and dozens of articles about what it is like being a psychologist.

Psychology Career Center
website: www.psychologycareercenter.org

Psychology Career Center is a free resource for psychology students that provides information about degree programs, internships, and career and salary information. Its website also includes news articles and information about psychology specialties.

Psychology.org
website: www.psychology.org

Psychology.org is an online resource for people interested in a career in psychology. It contains detailed information about degree programs and careers, as well as a collection of articles, videos, and other resources that discuss advances in the field of psychology.

Nurse

What Does a Nurse Do?

Samantha Narog wakes at 5:15 a.m. to prepare for her twelve-hour nursing shift at Memorial Sloan Kettering Cancer Center in Manhattan, New York. Before the day is done, she has distributed medication and collected blood for lab work, updated computer records, discharged several patients and admitted several others, sent patients for tests, and consulted with doctors and other nurses. She has also removed a catheter (a plastic tube that helps patients urinate) from one patient and inserted a drain (a tube that removes fluids from the body) into another, and she still found time to make sure the people under her care understood everything that was happening to them. "During these twelve hours, I was able to calm someone's fears about their newly placed drain," she wrote in a July 2017 article published in the blog *Calling All Nurses*. "I was also able to spend time getting to know patients and explain the steps of the day to them. . . . This keeps them from becoming frustrated because they now know things take time and they aren't just forgotten."

At a Glance

Nurse

Minimum Educational Requirements
Completion of accredited nursing program

Personal Qualities
Critical-thinking skills, high stress tolerance, strong interpersonal skills, compassion

Certification and Licensing
Required

Working Conditions
Hospital, clinic, or home setting

Salary Range
About $32,000 to $175,000

Number of Jobs
About 3,641,300

Future Job Outlook
Growth much faster than average

Narog wrote that, at the end of a long shift, "I leave with the feeling I did my best and I'm ready to come back tomorrow."

Narog is a registered nurse (RN) with a specialty certification in the treatment of cancer. Nurses like Narog who work in a hospital have many different roles: Some staff the emergency room, some assist doctors with surgical procedures, some treat infants or children, and some work in hospital offices or supervise other nurses. Outside of the hospital setting, nurses can care for people in their homes or for children at schools, work in nursing homes or free clinics, and even serve in the military. In addition, nurses can specialize in everything from pediatrics to end-of-life care. Those with advanced training can care for pregnant women and deliver babies, perform simple surgical procedures and administer anesthesia, teach at universities, or have patients of their own. In other words, a person considering a career in nursing has many options to choose from—which is one of the reasons a 2016 survey conducted by *U.S. News & World Report* found that RNs ranked number six and nurse practitioners ranked number four in its 100 Best Jobs list.

There are three main types of nurses: licensed practical nurses (LPNs), RNs, and advanced practice registered nurses (APRNs). LPNs have the least amount of training and therefore have the most restrictions on what types of care they can provide. In general, LPNs monitor vital signs, change bandages, administer some treatments, maintain records, and keep their patients comfortable while offering them emotional support. They are usually not permitted to insert IVs (intravenous hookups), supervise staff, or perform other advanced duties.

LPNs are usually supervised by RNs, who are responsible for coordinating all patient care. RNs carry out a doctor's treatment orders, give medication, take blood and perform other tests and procedures, and facilitate communication between doctor and patient. RNs often specialize in certain populations or disorders, and many have earned advanced certifications that allow them to take on more responsibility and earn higher salaries.

APRNs are RNs who have received additional specialized training. One type of APRN is a nurse anesthetist, who assists or takes the place of an anesthesiologist during surgical procedures. Nurse midwives are APRNs who can provide prenatal and wellness care to pregnant women, deliver babies, and manage emergency situations during labor. Clinical nurse specialists are APRNs who specialize in various areas, such as mental health or pediatrics. Finally, the most common type of APRN is a nurse practitioner. Nurse practitioners can do most of what a doctor can do—they can order and interpret tests, diagnose illnesses, prescribe medication, and offer primary care to patients without supervision by a physician.

How Do You Become a Nurse?

Education

Nurses train in specialized nursing programs at universities, hospitals, or accredited nursing schools. Many of these programs are quite competitive, in part because nursing schools have not kept up with the increased demand for nurses. The American Association of Colleges of Nursing reports that in 2016, US nursing schools turned away over sixty-four thousand qualified applicants because of budget and other shortfalls. To ensure a spot in nursing school, high school students should take classes in biology, chemistry, and math and maintain a high grade point average.

Each type of nursing certification requires a different level of education. LPNs need only to complete a one-year accredited program, in which they learn basic nursing skills, medical terminology, and basic pharmacology. Students who plan to become RNs have several educational options. They can earn an associate's degree in nursing from a local community college or training institute, which typically takes two years. These students often have to take additional classes in order to pass the RN licensing exam. They can complete a three-year diploma program, which offers a more in-depth education. Finally, they can complete a four-year bachelor of science program in nursing. RNs with bachelor's degrees often earn higher salaries and qualify for more in-depth certification programs. Some workplaces have tuition reimbursement programs that help LPNs become RNs or help RNs earn their bachelor's degree while they are employed.

RNs who want to advance their careers can pursue a master's degree. These two-year programs require students to take in-depth courses in anatomy, physiology, and pharmacology. A master's is required for entry into an advanced practice program. Another option for advanced study is the doctor of nursing practice degree (DNP) or a PhD in nursing.

Certification and Licensing

After completing an accredited nursing program, students must pass a licensing exam. Nurses are also required to have completed a specified number of hours working in clinical settings under supervision. In addition, they must submit to a background check, which includes a criminal history check, to demonstrate their professional fitness. A criminal history does not necessarily disqualify a person from becoming a nurse, but withholding information about past offenses often does. Each state has its own requirements for licensure, but all states use the same exam for LPNs and RNs.

RNs can earn certification credentials in dozens of specialties, such as medical-surgical nursing, informatics, pediatrics, or forensics. APRNs can also specialize in areas such as advanced diabetes management, emergency care, or psychiatric care.

Volunteer Work and Internships

High school students interested in becoming nurses can volunteer at local hospitals or clinics. Young people who are at least sixteen years old can also become certified nursing assistants, which may qualify them for a volunteer or paid internship.

Some student nurses supplement their training by becoming volunteer emergency medical technicians—the first responders who staff ambulances and provide emergency medical care. While EMTs must be at least eighteen years old, most states allow students younger than eighteen to take classes. In addition, many localities have junior EMT programs that allow high school students to assist EMTs.

Skills and Personality

Nurses must be levelheaded, focused, and able to multitask. They must also have strong analytical abilities and be detail oriented. Misreading an order, forgetting to complete a procedure, or overlooking a symptom can have deadly results. In addition, because many nurses deal with emergencies daily, they must be able to work well under stress.

Nurses also must have strong interpersonal skills and be compassionate. Showing patients compassion is not always easy—nurses often deal with patients who are angry, afraid, or in great pain. The best nurses can feel compassion for all people in distress yet not be upset by poor treatment at the hands of a suffering patient or frightened family member.

On the Job

Employers

More than half of all nurses are employed by hospitals. They are also employed by residential care facilities, physicians' offices, and outpatient clinics. Some nurses work for agencies that care for people in their homes, while others work for the government, supervising health care programs. Nurses can also be employed by large corporations, schools, community centers, or the military. Many nurse practitioners are self-employed and have their own practices.

Travel nurses are employed by agencies that place nurses in areas where there are not enough health care workers. Travel nurses complete placements that last anywhere from a few weeks to a year. They usually have their travel and living expenses paid by their employers and can earn twice as much as other nurses.

Working Conditions

Some nurses work in clinical settings, while others visit people in their homes. Nurses who work in hospitals usually work shifts that are ten to twelve hours long. Nurses who work in doctor's offices usually keep regular business hours.

A nurse makes sure her young patient is resting comfortably. A nurse's workday might include distributing medications to patients, inserting or removing catheters, updating computer records, and consulting with doctors and other medical staff.

Nurses are usually on their feet for most of the day, and some are required to lift or move patients. This puts them at risk for injury. In addition, nurses are regularly exposed to infectious diseases, hazardous drugs and chemicals, and sharp instruments. Patients who are frightened or mentally unstable can also pose a danger. To keep themselves safe, it is important that nurses always follow the safety guidelines put in place by their health care facility.

Earnings

According to the Bureau of Labor Statistics (BLS), in 2016 the median salary for LPNs was $44,090, with the lowest-paid 10 percent earning less than $32,510 and the highest-paid 10 percent earning more than $60,420. The median salary for RNs was $68,450, with the lowest-paid 10 percent earning less than $47,120 and the highest-paid 10 percent earning more than $102,990. The median salary for APRNs was $107,460, with the lowest-paid 10 percent earning less than $74,300 and the highest-paid 10 percent earning more than $175,170.

Opportunities for Advancement

There are ample opportunities for nurses to advance their careers. Education and certification are the key to advancement. With certification, nurses can move into supervisory or administrative positions, lead research projects or head governmental programs, or teach in nursing programs. In addition, some nurses decide to go to medical school and become doctors.

What Is the Future Outlook for Nurses?

The BLS reports that all types of nurses will see a much faster-than-average growth in employment. From 2014 to 2024, employment of LPNs and RNs is expected to grow by 16 percent, and employment of APRNs is expected to grow by 31 percent.

The demand for qualified nurses is outpacing supply. The American Nurses Association reports that nearly seven hundred thousand nurses are projected to retire or leave the labor force by 2024, and nursing schools are currently not graduating enough nurses to replace them. In addition, a majority of the population will be elderly, which will only increase the demand for nurses in the coming decade.

Not only are nurses in short supply, they are also taking on more responsibility. According to a July 2017 article on the Athena Career Academy website:

> Due in part to a shortage of doctors in many areas of the United States, nurses have accordingly been granted expanded responsibilities in many fields. This makes nursing more appealing, more valuable, and more necessary across the country. . . . eMedical facilities looking to keep up with the growth of the medical industry will look for more nurses, not more doctors—because hiring doctors to keep up simply won't be feasible.

This is just one more reason why nursing will remain one of the top health care careers for the foreseeable future.

Find Out More

All Nursing Schools
website: www.allnursingschools.com

All Nursing Schools is a website that features a comprehensive online directory of nursing programs in the United States. It includes information about financial aid, fields of study, and current salary and job growth data for all branches of nursing and nursing specialties.

American Nurses Association (ANA)
8515 Georgia Ave., Suite 400
Silver Spring, MD 20919
website: www.nursingworld.org

The ANA is a professional organization that works to advance the nursing profession. Its website has detailed information about what nurses do, how to become a nurse, and how to apply and prepare for nursing school. It also contains a career center and a community discussion forum.

DiscoverNursing.com
website: www.discovernursing.com

DiscoverNursing.com is a website created by Johnson & Johnson to address the nursing shortage and help recruit nurses into the profession. The website is designed for students interested in nursing and contains information about schools, scholarships, and career options.

EveryNurse.org
2926 Juniper St.
San Diego, CA 92104
website: www.everynurse.org

EveryNurse.org is a nursing career research website that includes career descriptions, interviews, licensing information, and employer profiles. It has a series of day-in-the-life videos for various types of nurses, as well as details about specific educational and licensing requirements.

Paramedic

In 2016 Nate Boyce, a newly certified paramedic working in Colorado Springs, got a call to rescue a young man who had fallen 60 feet (18.3 m) while rock climbing. As Boyce told Zach Sokol in an October 2016 interview published in *Vice*, the man was "the definition of broken." Boyce's team administered pain medication to the man, stabilized him, and moved him off the mountain to an emergency transport helicopter. As a paramedic, Boyce is qualified to care for people with severe injuries. "We provide surprisingly advanced care," he told Sokol. "Not only do we have the ability to treat really life-threatening illnesses, but we make people feel better. Treating people's pain is awesome."

Paramedics are a type of emergency medical technician (EMT) with advanced medical training. They staff emergency medical services (EMS) transport vehicles, such as ambulances and helicopters. Unless there is a doctor or nurse on the transport vehicle, paramedics are the ranking members of an EMS team. Their job is to assess

At a Glance

Paramedic

Minimum Educational Requirements
Completion of a paramedic training program

Personal Qualities
Ability to think critically under extreme stress, strong communication and interpersonal skills

Certification and Licensing
Required

Working Conditions
Indoor and outdoor emergency situations

Salary Range
About $33,000 to $78,000

Number of Jobs
About 97,400

Future Job Outlook
Much faster than average

the condition of patients, stabilize them, and transport them to the nearest medical facility.

Unlike most EMTs, who need only a few hundred hours of training to become certified, paramedics train for two years. They are qualified to do complex medical procedures, such as inserting an airway tube into the windpipe of a patient who is not breathing, administering powerful medications, stitching wounds, performing blood transfusions, and interpreting complex diagnostic tests. They are also trained to relay patient information quickly and accurately to emergency health care staff. Many people compare paramedics to nurses. Although they are trained in different areas, their knowledge and skills are roughly equivalent.

Paramedics work at emergency services centers, which can be stand-alone ambulance companies, divisions of hospitals attached to the emergency department, or fire stations. Many paramedics are also firefighters, and like firefighters, they work shifts that are twelve to forty-eight hours in length. During their shifts, they live at their workplace so that they can respond immediately to calls. While on duty they inventory the ambulance, maintain equipment, practice procedures, perform emergency drills, and complete administrative paperwork. Since paramedics are usually the ranking health care providers at an EMS station, they will often train and supervise volunteer and paid EMTs.

Most people become paramedics because they want to save lives. However, they soon learn that most of what a paramedic does is routine—and not very exciting. On a typical shift, an EMS team might transport a patient from a hospital to a long-term care facility, help an elderly person who has fallen, and staff a first aid station for a community event. The team may also arrive at a residence and find a person who has a minor injury that could easily be treated by a family doctor, or a person who has had too much alcohol and has become belligerent. As most paramedics will attest, calls that are true emergencies are the exception. This can be extremely disappointing to people who enter emergency services looking for an exciting career. However, in true emergencies, quick action from paramedics can be the difference between life and death. These first responders are highly trained health care professionals who provide a crucial service to the community.

How Do You Become a Paramedic?

Education

Paramedics must have completed basic and advanced EMT training before they can enroll in a paramedic training program. An EMT basic certification requires about 150 hours of instruction, and an EMT advanced certification requires about 400 hours of instruction. In addition, some training programs require students to have worked as an EMT for a certain length of time. Students interested in becoming paramedics should take math and science courses in high school, including advanced algebra, biology, and chemistry. Many paramedic programs require that specific math and science courses have been completed in high school.

Paramedic programs are offered at community colleges and technical schools. These programs involve about twelve hundred hours of instruction, take about two years to complete, and often result in an associate's degree. Each state has different educational requirements, but associate's degree programs require that paramedics take college-level biology, math, and English courses in addition to courses in advanced lifesaving procedures. Students typically complete a combination of classroom instruction, clinical hours in a hospital or other health care facility, and field internships. They learn to assess patients, deliver medications and lifesaving interventions, provide safe transport to patients, and communicate effectively with medical professionals and the public. Examples of courses in a typical paramedic program include critical trauma care, advanced cardiac life support, and advanced pediatric care.

Certification and Licensing

All paramedics must be licensed by the state in which they work. To become licensed, some states require that paramedics be certified by the National Registry of Emergency Medical Technicians (NREMT), while others have their own requirements and examinations. The NREMT certification exam has two parts. The first part is a written exam that tests a candidate's knowledge. The second is a practical exam that tests the candidate's ability to assess patients, perform lifesaving procedures, manage a team, and communicate with other health care professionals. Certification expires after two years, and paramedics must take continuing education courses to become recertified.

Volunteer Work and Internships

Paramedics usually start out as volunteer ambulance drivers or EMTs before they pursue paid work in emergency services or enroll in a paramedic training program. High school students interested in becoming paramedics can join junior EMT programs at their local fire departments, hospitals, or emergency services stations. Most of these programs require that students maintain a certain minimum grade point average, have a clean driving record, and pass a drug-screening test. Some junior EMT programs allow their volunteers to ride along in ambulances as observers, participate in training drills, help maintain the equipment and stock the ambulances, and even help assess patients and provide basic first aid.

Skills and Personality

Paramedics must be able to assess and diagnose a patient quickly and accurately. This takes strong problem-solving and deductive-reasoning skills. It also requires the ability to listen carefully to a patient so as not to miss a crucial piece of information. Paramedics must be able to do this under extreme stress. No matter what the emergency, they must remain calm and levelheaded at all times.

While paramedics must be compassionate, it is important that they not let their emotions affect the care they give to patients. As Boyce explained, "Our goal is to never have emotions affect the way you do things. That's like a [tenet] of medicine: You treat everyone the same way regardless of your connection to them." However, as he explained to Sokol, it took him a while to learn how to keep his emotions in check. "When you're really new you're afraid that everyone in the ambulance is gonna die," he told Sokol. "You're feeling is that, like, *I'm on an ambulance—this is life and death stuff. It could be any second that this person who just called me for leg pain just drops dead!* Over time you get over that because it just doesn't happen like that very often."

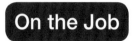

Employers

Paramedics are employed by local governments, private ambulance services, and hospitals. Some work on medical helicopters or airplanes to transport critically injured people to hospitals. Others put their skills to use in the military, while others serve on national and local emergency response teams.

Working Conditions

Paramedics work indoors and outdoors, sometimes in dangerous locations, such as accident sites, crime scenes, or natural disasters. They are required to carry heavy equipment, bend and kneel, and lift patients onto stretchers. They can be exposed to infectious diseases or injured by patients who are violent.

Paramedics work shifts that last twelve to forty-eight hours. Most work full time, and many work more than forty hours a week. Shifts are staggered to ensure that all hours are covered, so paramedics can expect to work nights, holidays, and weekends.

Earnings

The Bureau of Labor Statistics (BLS) tracks the salary of EMTs and paramedics together, so it does not provide a pay range for this position. According to the website Salary.com, paramedics made an average salary of $40,795 in 2017, with the lowest-paid 10 percent earning $32,843 and the highest-paid 10 percent earning $51,679. A 2015 survey by the *Journal of Emergency Medical Services* found that on average, paramedics made $53,160 in the public sector and $44,953 in the private sector. *U.S. News & World Report* notes that Tacoma, Washington, has the highest average salary for paramedics at $77,770.

Paramedics assist a man and young boy who were injured in a terrorist attack in New York City in October 2017. Paramedics treat both small and life-threatening injuries and stabilize patients until they can be seen by a doctor.

Most paramedics believe they are underpaid for the job that they do. This is because a paramedic receives about the same amount of training as a registered nurse (RN), yet an RN's job—which has a much higher average salary—is less physically demanding and dangerous and has a better work-life balance. This may be why paramedics tend to leave the profession after only four years on average. As Boyce explained, "I can't emphasize how terrible the pay is. . . . We have so many people leave the industry who are good at their jobs. They interact with the rest of healthcare professionals who are well-compensated, and they're like, . . . "Why shouldn't I just go to nursing school and make twice as much money for significantly less responsibility?"

One reason that paramedics do not make as much as other health care professionals is that EMTs—who receive significantly less training—can handle most EMS calls. EMTs make a much lower salary than paramedics, and many are volunteers. This undervalues the service paramedics provide.

Opportunities for Advancement

To advance in their careers, paramedics can become supervisors or directors of emergency services organizations or instructors in paramedic training programs. Some become tactical paramedics— paramedics trained to accompany law enforcement into emergency situations. Others join the military and work as medics. In general, however, there are few opportunities for advancement within this field, which may be another reason most paramedics move on to other careers after a few years. Some move into sales of emergency medical equipment, some become firefighters, and some enter related health care fields, becoming nurses, physician assistants, or doctors.

What Is the Future Outlook for Paramedics?

The BLS projects that employment of EMTs and paramedics will grow by 24 percent from 2014 to 2024, much faster than average. This is due in part to a growth in the elderly population, which tends to have more health emergencies than younger populations.

Because the BLS combines statistics for paramedics with all EMTs, it is unclear how many paramedic positions are available nationwide. However, the NREMT reports that as of April 2017, there were 97,365 nationally certified paramedics in the United States, with an unemployment rate of only 2.6 percent. In addition, the NREMT reports that many localities across the country have seen enrollment numbers in paramedic programs drop, and many paramedic positions remain unfilled. This means that there should be no job shortage for paramedics in the future. Virtually every qualified paramedic should be able to find employment.

Find Out More

EMS Daily News
website: www.emsdailynews.com

EMS Daily News is an online news source that compiles national and international news stories, articles, and blog posts related to

EMS. Its website has an extensive library of articles that will give those interested in becoming a paramedic information about the ways EMS professionals work within their communities.

EMS.gov

National Highway Traffic Safety Administration
Office of Emergency Medical Services
1200 New Jersey Ave. SE
Washington, DC 20590
website: www.ems.gov

EMS.gov is the website of the National Highway Traffic Safety Administration's Office of Emergency Medical Services, which supports national EMS systems, projects, and research. The website contains data and statistics, reports about EMS, webinars, and the newsletter *EMS Update*.

National Association of Emergency Medical Technicians (NAEMT)

PO Box 1400
Clinton, MS 39060
website: www.naemt.org

The NAEMT is a nonprofit organization that supports and educates EMTs, paramedics, first responders, and other professionals working in prehospital emergency medicine. Its website includes descriptions of its various education programs and has detailed information about how to pursue a career as a paramedic.

Paramedic.com

website: www.paramedic.com

Paramedic.com is a clearinghouse for news, education, and job opportunities for paramedics. Its website features the MedicCast podcast, which discusses medical care, emergency procedures, and day-to-day advice for EMS professionals. It also features ParamedicTV, a series of videos featuring medical and emergency techniques and other topics related to careers in paramedicine.

Family Practitioner

What Does a Family Practitioner Do?

A pediatrician is a doctor who specializes in the treatment of children. An internal medicine physician, or internist, is a doctor who treats only adults. But if members of a family want to use the same doctor for everyone's medical needs, they see a family practitioner, also known as a family practice physician or family doctor.

Family practitioners treat people at all stages of life. As primary care physicians, they are usually the first health care providers people seek out when they are sick. They also coordinate all of their patients' care, helping them navigate through a health care system that can be complicated and confusing.

Family medicine is different from other medical specialties in several ways. First, family practitioners must be skilled in all aspects of medicine and be able to serve all populations. Trained in everything from obstetrics to geriatrics, they can care for a pregnant woman, deliver a baby, and diagnose and treat the disorders and diseases of childhood, adolescence, adulthood, and old age. Many do simple surgical procedures and screening tests, and most continue to treat

At a Glance

Family Practitioner

Minimum Educational Requirements
Doctor of medicine degree, three-year residency

Personal Qualities
Excellent critical-thinking and interpersonal skills, compassion

Certification and Licensing
License required; certifications optional

Working Conditions
Clinical settings

Salary Range
About $69,000 to $340,000

Number of Jobs
About 123,000

Future Job Outlook
Growth much faster than average

their patients if they are admitted to the hospital. And unlike other specialists, the scope of their training allows them to diagnose a wide variety of disorders and diseases. Many medical students choose this area of practice because they enjoy variety and the challenges it brings.

The second way family practitioners differ from other kinds of doctors is that they develop long-term relationships with their patients, especially if they work in private practice. Those relationships are at the heart of their practice. Knowing people well allows family practitioners to consider their patients' work-life balance and stressors, their living situations, and their relationships when making a diagnosis or prescribing a treatment. And because they get to know their patients, they often can spot a change in health status that a specialist might miss. Typically, doctors choose to specialize in family medicine because they believe that developing these relationships is the key to providing good health care. And maintaining these relationships long term is usually what gives them the most satisfaction. As Dr. Russell Kohl said in an October 2015 article on the American Academy of Family Physicians (AAFP) website, "To deliver a baby that you have already cared for in utero and then to watch them grow and succeed has been the most rewarding part of my practice."

Medical students who choose to specialize in family medicine have an unusually large number of options when it comes to how to practice their specialty. Many join medical groups or open solo practices that offer primary care, but some choose to be hospitalists, which means that they work primarily in a hospital. Others focus on emergency medicine and work in urgent care centers. Ernest Brown, a family practitioner in Washington, DC, does only house calls. "I can go through the cupboards, see what the medications are," he explained to Eun Kyung Kim in an August 2017 article on the *Today* show's website. "I can look around, I can smell things, check the refrigerator, see how they're eating. I can do more in one house call than I could ever do sitting in a box at a clinic, being told I have to see patients every 10 minutes."

Family practitioners who work in rural areas often do more procedures and offer more services than those who work in urban areas, where there are more resources. Some deliver babies, perform surgical procedures, set broken bones, or care for patients with terminal diseases. Some family practitioners specialize in sports medicine and offer services to their local sports teams, while others specialize in disaster relief, working in areas with few resources or that have been struck by a natural disaster. Family practitioners can also serve in the military, offering their services on military bases to the families that live there. Finally, some use the breadth of their knowledge to advance public health. They work on research projects, guide task forces to combat disease, or act as medical directors in county or state health departments.

How Do You Become a Family Practitioner?

Education

Becoming a medical doctor is a huge commitment of time and money. It takes at least eleven years of higher education and training after high school to become a family practitioner. In high school, students should focus on math and science classes, especially biology and chemistry.

Doing well as an undergraduate is crucial to getting accepted to medical school, a four-year graduate school that all would-be doctors must attend. Many undergraduate programs have a premedical, or premed, track—a series of courses that prepare students to take the Medical College Admission Test (MCAT), a standardized test that is required for admission to medical schools in the United States. Students do not have to be on the premed track to be accepted to medical school; however, medical schools do require that students have completed specific courses in math and science. Completing the required courses, doing well on the MCAT, getting good grades, and participating in activities that demonstrate a commitment to medicine are all determining factors for whether a student is accepted to medical school.

In medical school, a student's first two years are spent in the classroom and the second two years in a hospital or other clinical setting. During the second two years, students receive training in a variety of medical specialties. They also begin applying for a residency program. Residency programs in family medicine allow newly graduated doctors to continue their training under the supervision of licensed physicians. Residents work for three years in a family practice setting. During this time, they continue to train in various specialty areas, such as obstetrics, pediatrics, general surgery, and emergency medicine. Doctors who want additional or expanded training can enter a dual-degree residency program in emergency medicine, internal medicine, or psychiatry. These dual-degree residencies take five years instead of three.

After completing a residency, doctors can attend a specialty training program called a fellowship. Fellowships available to family medicine physicians include rural medicine, geriatrics, medical research, or sports medicine. Fellowships in family medicine usually last one year.

Certification and Licensing

Doctors must be licensed in order to practice medicine. The licensing process for doctors is complex and varies from state to state, but all states require doctors to pass standardized written and oral exams. During medical school and residency, students take a three-part exam called the United States Medical Licensing Examination (USMLE). They take the first part of the USMLE at the end of their second year of medical school, the second part during their fourth year, and the third after their first year of residency. Once they have passed all three parts of the USMLE and have completed all requirements for their residency, they may apply for a medical license.

After completing the residency, the doctor is eligible to take the family medicine board certification exam, which will make them board certified in family medicine. Board certification is not necessary to practice family medicine, but it allows doctors to present themselves to the public as family medicine specialists. Doctors must become recertified every eight years.

Board-certified family practitioners can also earn certificates of added qualification (CAQs). CAQs are available in five areas: adolescent medicine, geriatric medicine, hospice and palliative medicine, sleep medicine, and sports medicine.

Volunteer Work and Internships

High school students interested in becoming family practitioners can gain experience in the health care field by volunteering at a local hospital or clinic. Students who are age sixteen or older can train to be a certified nursing assistant, which may qualify them for a volunteer or paid internship.

Skills and Personality

Family practitioners must have excellent critical-thinking and problem-solving skills to excel at diagnosing their patients. They also must have compassion, be excellent listeners, and have strong interpersonal skills so that they can build long-lasting relationships with the families they serve.

Like all physicians, family practitioners must have strong academic skills and a drive to succeed to complete the taxing educational requirements necessary to become a doctor. These traits will also help them keep abreast of the latest developments in their field, assuring that they provide the best care to their patients.

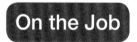

On the Job

Employers

Many family practitioners are in private practice or have teamed up with other doctors to form a group practice. This means that these doctors are also business owners and are responsible for all aspects of their practice. Other family practitioners are employed by hospitals, nursing homes, community health centers or clinics, urgent care centers, or large entities like corporations or universities that have their own health care centers.

Working Conditions

Most family practitioners split their time between a traditional office and a clinical setting, such as an exam room or hospital ward. Family practitioners tend to work long hours, but unlike other specialties, they spend a lot of time with their patients. They often must be on call for emergency situations on a rotating basis, which can mean speaking to patients over the phone or meeting them at the hospital at night or on weekends.

Earnings

Traditionally, family practitioners earn less than some other medical specialties. However, because of the high demand for family practitioners, the average annual salary has been on the rise. Merritt Hawkins, a health care recruiting agency, found in a 2016 survey that salaries for family medicine had increased by 13 percent. According to the Bureau of Labor Statistics (BLS), the average salary for family practitioners in 2016 was about $200,810 per year, and salaries ranged from about $69,000 to $340,000. Earnings in rural areas tend to be higher due to increased demand. A 2016 study by the Medicus Firm found that family practitioners in rural areas earned an average of $227,261 per year.

Opportunities for Advancement

Family practitioners advance by gaining experience or building their practice over time. Earning CAQs or taking part in notable research studies can also increase the salary they can command. This can help them be promoted to more senior positions within their practice group or hospital. Some experienced family practitioners also take faculty positions in medical schools.

What Is the Future Outlook for Family Practitioners?

The BLS projects that employment of all physicians and surgeons will grow by 14 percent from 2014 to 2024, much faster than average. This is partly because of a general increase in the aged population, which tends to need more health care, and an overall shortage of doctors in the United States. There has also been a trend to reward doctors on the basis of patient outcomes instead of services performed. Because family practitioners can make the most difference in a patient's overall health, they are reaping the benefits of this trend.

The AAFP confirms that the demand for family practitioners is also growing at a fast pace. It reports that in a 2016 survey Merritt Hawkins found that family physicians were the most recruited type of doctor—and that they had been for the past eight years. "We are the No. 1 career opportunity in medicine and the one discipline where you can take care of complex patients across all organ systems and both genders," wrote AAFP president Dr. Wanda Filer in a June 17, 2016, article on the AAFP website. "You will always have a job as a family physician."

Find Out More

American Academy of Family Physicians (AAFP)
11400 Tomahawk Creek Pkwy.
Leawood, KS 66211-2680
website: https://nf.aafp.org

The AAFP is a medical organization that promotes family medicine. Its website has a section devoted to educating students about career options in family medicine and how to become a family doctor.

Association of American Medical Colleges (AAMC)
655 K St. NW, Suite 100
Washington, DC 20001
website: https://students-residents.aamc.org

The AAMC is a nonprofit association of medical colleges in the United States. Its web page for students provides comprehensive information about choosing a medical career, applying to and attending medical school, and choosing and completing a residency in family medicine.

Mom MD
website: www.mommd.com

Mom MD is devoted to helping women who want to become physicians or who already have careers in medicine. Its website contains articles, blogs, forums, and other resources of interest to these women, as well as specific information about becoming a family practitioner.

Society of Teachers of Family Medicine (STFM)
11400 Tomahawk Creek Pkwy., Suite 240
Leawood, KS 66211
website: www.stfm.org

The STFM is a professional organization that promotes teachers of family medicine. Its website contains resources for students interested in a career in family medicine, information about residency programs, news and journal articles, and an online career resource.

Dental Hygienist

What Does a Dental Hygienist Do?

Maria Khan came to America from Pakistan for her last year of high school. She wanted to be a dentist, but her family could not afford the enormous expense involved in going to dental school. Instead, she enrolled in the dental hygienist program at Hostos Community College in New York City. Now, at twenty-three years old, she is earning forty-five dollars an hour as a dental hygienist, more than most medical technicians and nurses. She also has weekends off and can afford to finish her bachelor's degree, which she is doing part time. Best of all, Khan loves her job. "I love helping people and seeing the smile on their face when they tell me I gave them the best cleaning," she told Heather Long of CNNMoney in an April 2017 article.

The primary job of a dental hygienist is to clean teeth by removing tartar and plaque with manual, power, and ultrasonic tools. Hygienists also check the health of a patient's teeth, mouth, and jaw; take X-rays; and report their findings to the dentist for whom they work. Dental hygienists also treat gum disease and apply seal-

At a Glance

Dental Hygienist

Minimum Educational Requirements
Associate's degree

Personal Qualities
Critical thinking, detail oriented, dexterity, good interpersonal skills

Certification and Licensing
Required

Working Conditions
Indoors in clinical settings

Salary Range
About $50,900 to $100,200

Number of Jobs
About 200,500

Future Job Outlook
Growth much faster than average

ants and fluoride to help protect teeth. They are responsible for educating their patients about proper oral hygiene by showing them how to brush and floss and advising them about diet and nutrition as it relates to mouth health. Finally, they document their findings within the dentist's patient records, which are almost always computerized.

Being a dental hygienist is one of the highest-paid jobs in the United States that does not require a four-year college degree. Opportunities for dental hygienists are expanding at a rapid pace, and the Bureau of Labor Statistics (BLS) estimates that nearly forty thousand new hygienist jobs will be created by 2024. Students are taking notice, especially low-income and immigrant students, who can make enough in this career to enjoy a middle-class lifestyle without accumulating too much debt in student loans. Hostos's two-year program costs only $14,000, which includes books, equipment, and fees. Many of the students at Hostos are from poor or immigrant communities and are the first people in their families to go to college. One such student is Kendra Francilot, who grew up in Haiti and left after a devastating earthquake in 2010 killed an estimated three hundred thousand people. Francilot hopes that one day, after she graduates, she will be able to return to Haiti to open a clinic. At Hostos, she often works on people who come to the free clinic. "It's the greatest feeling when you make a difference for people," she told Long. "It's a job that makes you feel good."

The high pay and good work-life balance of dental hygienist careers is attracting not only poor and immigrant students, however. The field, which has traditionally been dominated by women, is now attracting men of all economic backgrounds. Even college graduates unable to find employment are going back to school to become dental hygienists. "We have students from Ivy League colleges here right now who are looking for a better career," Salim Rayman, head of the dental hygiene program at Hostos, told Long. According to Rayman, the reason is simple: "When [Hostos] students graduate, they can almost guarantee themselves a job."

How Do You Become a Dental Hygienist?

Education

To work as a dental hygienist, students must complete an associate's degree in dental hygiene. Dental hygiene programs usually take three years to complete and are available at community colleges, technical schools, and universities. Because most states license only hygienists who have attended an accredited program, students should check that their chosen program has been accredited by the Commission on Dental Accreditation.

Some programs require that students have completed a year of college before they are admitted to the program (that year counts toward their three-year degree requirements). Most colleges also require that all students receiving an associate's degree have taken classes in a wide variety of subjects, such as English, math, and science. Areas of study relating to dental hygiene include head and neck anatomy, nutrition, pathology, radiography, and periodontics (the dental specialty that focuses on the gums and other structures that support the teeth).

Students study dental hygiene in the classroom, laboratories, and clinical settings. In most programs they first practice cleaning teeth on special mannequins designed as teaching tools. Next, they practice on their classmates. Finally, they work on real patients. Some dental hygiene programs have a clinic where low-income people can get free cleanings done by students. If no patients are available, students are responsible for finding their own volunteers. "The hardest part is gathering all the patients you need to complete the training certification," Kevin Artis, class president at Hostos, told Long. Hostos requires students to work under careful supervision on at least sixteen patients with various types of dental issues.

Bachelor's and master's degrees are also available in dental hygiene. Students interested in teaching, research, or working for public health programs or other government entities will need at least a bachelor's degree in dental hygiene.

Certification and Licensing

All dental hygienists must be licensed by the state in which they practice. Requirements vary from state to state, but most require students to pass the National Board Dental Hygiene Examination in addition to a state exam. State exams have a practical component in which a candidate must demonstrate his or her clinical dental hygiene skills on real patients. After being awarded a state license, dental hygienists may refer to themselves as registered dental hygienists and may practice within that state.

A dental hygienist checks the health of her patient's gums and teeth. Hygienists clean teeth, take X-rays, apply sealants and fluoride, and discuss proper oral hygiene with their patients.

Volunteer Work and Internships

The best way to volunteer in this field is to help out in a free dental clinic. Volunteers can take medical histories, stock supplies, educate patients about dental care, work reception, or help calm frightened patients. High school students can also secure a summer internship in a dental office. Because some hygienist programs are competitive, prior experience in a clinic or dental office can improve one's chances of being accepted.

Volunteering or working at a summer internship is also a good way to see what dental hygienists do on the job. Working in dental hygiene is not for everyone—hygienists must work inside the mouths of their patients, so it is not a job for the squeamish. Volunteering can give prospective students a good idea of what their workdays will be like as a hygienist and help them decide whether it is the right career for them.

Skills and Personality

The most successful dental hygienists have strong people skills. They understand that many people are afraid of going to the dentist and that the work of a hygienist can be uncomfortable for them. In addition, some patients can get defensive or angry if they are told that they need to improve their dental hygiene routine. A good dental hygienist can offer advice and instruction in an encouraging way and will not be offended by the occasional difficult patient.

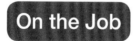

On the Job

Employers

Most dental hygienists are employed by dentists in group or solo practices. Those who work full time often work at more than one office. A small number of hygienists work in doctor's offices, in outpatient clinics, or at schools.

Traditionally, almost all dental hygienists had to be supervised by a dentist. However, many states are now considering allowing licensed hygienists to work in other settings without supervision. For instance, in 2017 Wisconsin passed a law that allowed licensed hygienists to work in clinics and community health centers that provide primary care to low-income patients. This will not only create many more jobs for hygienists, it will bring needed dental care to a historically underserved population.

Working Conditions

Dental hygienists work indoors in clinical settings, most frequently in dentists' offices. They spend long hours in positions that may strain the neck and back. They must wear safety glasses, surgical masks, and gloves to protect themselves from diseases that may be present in the blood or saliva of their patients. They work with sharp instruments that have the potential to cause injury. They also take X-rays, which normally poses very little risk of radiation exposure to the controller.

Earnings

The BLS reports that in 2016, the median annual wage for dental hygienists was $72,910 for full-time employment. The lowest-paid 10 percent earned less than $50,870, and the highest-paid 10 percent earned more than $100,170. Dental hygienists who work for a dental practice full time often receive benefits, such as health insurance and vacation time. However, since many dentists need the services of a hygienist only a few days a week, many hygienists work for more than one dentist and may not qualify for benefits. In addition, about half of all dental hygienists work part time.

Most dental hygienists get a standard or hourly rate; however, many dentists' offices now offer hygienists a commission for selling certain services. "The trend now is commission based salaries," Rayman told Long. "You get a flat rate for your work, but you earn more on top of that if you sell certain things in the office." Hygienists often recommend teeth whitening, teeth straightening, or teeth veneers to their patients.

Opportunities for Advancement

The more experience dental hygienists accumulate, the higher rate they can command. Dentists appreciate skilled hygienists who can spot cavities or other problems. Hygienists who can assist dentists with procedures from time to time are also in demand. Finally, it is extremely important to have a good rapport with patients. Dental hygienists who have a good reputation with their patients enhance a dentist's practice, which makes them more desirable as employees.

Dental hygienists can also increase their earning potential by taking continuing education courses or by getting a bachelor's or master's degree. Those who want to move away from direct patient care can use their degree to get jobs in management, education, administration, public health, or research. For instance, a hygienist with a bachelor's degree can get a job managing a government program in public health. Hygienists with master's degrees can become dental hygiene professors or work in dental health research.

What Is the Future Outlook for Dental Hygienists?

The BLS projects that employment will grow by 19 percent from 2014 to 2024, a rate that is much faster than average. This is partially because the aging population is projected to increase, and teeth tend to need more care as a person gets older. In addition, advances in dentistry and knowledge about dental hygiene will result in more people keeping their teeth as they age.

However, it is important to note that as demand increases, the number of new graduates from dental hygiene programs is also increasing. This will result in strong competition in the labor force. Hygienists with the most experience will likely have the best job prospects.

Find Out More

American Dental Association (ADA)
211 E. Chicago Ave.
Chicago, IL 60611-2678
website: www.ada.org

The ADA is the largest professional dental association in the United States. Its website has information about the education and training requirements of dental hygienists, as well as dozens of articles related to dental hygienist careers.

American Dental Hygienists Association (ADHA)
444 N. Michigan Ave., Suite 400
Chicago, IL 60611
website: www.adha.org

The ADHA is the largest professional organization for dental hygienists in the United States. Its website includes information about dental hygiene programs, scholarships and grants, career paths, licensure, and current job opportunities.

Commission on Dental Accreditation (CODA)
211 E. Chicago Ave.
Chicago, IL 60611
website: www.ada.org/en/coda

CODA's website contains a comprehensive list of all accredited programs in dental education, including dental hygiene. Listings have links to the 331 individual programs accredited in the United States and Canada.

Dentistry iQ
website: www.dentistryiq.com

Dentistry iQ is a comprehensive resource for dental professionals. It has a section devoted to dental hygienists that contains information on career development, current salary information, and dozens of articles and videos for students interested in becoming dental hygienists.

Pharmacist

What Does a Pharmacist Do?

Pharmacists are experts in the use and effects of drugs and medications. They provide patients with medications that have been prescribed by the patients' physicians and advise them on safe and proper use of those medications. They are also responsible for making sure that the drugs they dispense will not negatively interact with any other drugs the patients are taking or any medical conditions the patients have. While there are now computer programs designed to catch such interactions, they are not always accurate, which is why pharmacists must be well versed in the effects of a wide variety of medications. Pharmacists must also keep strict inventory records, supervise and manage pharmacy technicians, and be well versed in the computer programs and databases used by pharmacies.

As health care professionals who are accessible to the public without an appointment, pharmacists play an important role in the community. They conduct wellness screenings, provide immunizations, and can advise patients about healthy lifestyle choices. According to a 2016 profile of pharmacist careers by the col-

At a Glance

Pharmacist

Minimum Educational Requirements
Doctoral degree

Personal Qualities
Strong analytical skills, detail oriented, good communication skills

Certification and Licensing
Required

Working Conditions
Indoors in a pharmacy or laboratory setting

Salary Range
About $87,000 to $158,000

Number of Jobs
About 297,100

Future Job Outlook
Slower than average

lege admissions services organization the Princeton Review, "It is an increasing part of the pharmacist's job to be actively involved with patients, providing information on prescription drugs, referring patients to appropriate over-the-counter drugs, and advising physicians on the proper selection and use of medications."

Some pharmacists mix ingredients into customized medications for their patients. This is called compounding. Compounding is a way to customize a patient's medication to meet his or her specific needs. For instance, some medications must be suspended in liquid and flavored so that they can be taken by young children or people with problems swallowing pills. Other medications must be dispensed in nonstandard dosages. While all pharmacists are trained in compounding, some specialize in this field. These pharmacists work in specialty compounding pharmacies or in pharmaceutical companies. According to the specialty compounding pharmacy United Pharmacy, pharmacists with advanced training in compounding are in high demand.

How Do You Become a Pharmacist?

Education

Pharmacists must have a doctor of pharmacy, or PharmD, degree. Just as medical doctors must go to medical school, pharmacists must complete an accredited pharmacist program. There are several ways to earn a PharmD. High school students who know they want to become pharmacists can apply directly to a pharmacy program that combines undergraduate and graduate education. These programs typically take six years to complete. The first two years are spent taking required undergraduate courses, while the last four years are spent taking graduate-level courses. Students graduate with both a bachelor's degree and a PharmD degree.

Other pharmacy programs offer only graduate courses. Students interested in these programs can complete their two years of required undergraduate courses at another college or university and then apply to the pharmacy program. Some of these graduate-level programs allow students to apply while they are

A pharmacist logs prescription information for later reference. Pharmacists provide patients with medications that have been prescribed by a doctor and advise them on safe and proper use of those medications.

in high school. These are called early assurance programs. High school students accepted to early assurance programs are guaranteed a spot in the program after they complete their undergraduate course work.

Finally, students can apply to a pharmacy program after earning a bachelor's degree. Students who decide while in college or after graduation to become pharmacists often go this route. Their undergraduate degree can be in any area, but they still will need to have completed the courses required by the pharmacy program. For this reason, it is crucial that students interested in a career as a pharmacist research the specific requirements of the pharmacy program they are interested in as soon as possible.

Pharmacy programs are competitive. Students applying to a pharmacy program directly out of high school will need good grades in science and math. Many programs have minimum requirements for grade point average and scores on the SAT. Some programs also require students to take the Pharmacy College Admission Test, which students often take while doing their undergraduate course work. Finally, most pharmacy programs require students to apply through a standardized application process called the Pharmacy College Application Service, or PharmCAS, which can be found online.

Pharmacy programs require students to take a variety of courses, such as organic chemistry, human anatomy, and pharmacy lab skills, as well as courses on how drugs are used to treat complex diseases such as cancer, or how immunizations prevent the spread of disease. In addition, students are required to complete internships in community and hospital pharmacies, getting hands-on experience under the supervision of licensed pharmacists.

After earning a PharmD degree, some graduates go on to get a PhD, a degree that allows pharmacists to do research for drug companies or teach at a university. In addition, PharmD graduates can do a two-year residency or fellowship in pharmacy practice or research.

Certification and Licensing

Pharmacists must be licensed in the state in which they practice. While states vary in their requirements, all require that students pass the North American Pharmacist Licensure Examination. States also require pharmacists to take either the Multistate

Pharmacy Jurisprudence Examination or an equivalent exam that tests the student's knowledge of pharmacy law. In addition, each state requires that students have a certain number of hours of practical experience (usually completed during a student's internship). Most states also require that candidates submit to a criminal background check. Because pharmacists work with controlled substances, many states do not allow applicants with certain criminal histories to become licensed pharmacists.

Volunteer Work and Internships

Pharmacy internships are usually reserved for pharmacy students. However, some pharmacies have programs for high school students interested in becoming pharmacists. For instance, the national chain Walgreens has a pharmacy technician job-shadow program for high school students. This program allows students to see what it is like to work in a retail pharmacy and interact with the pharmacists and technicians. Because of the legal restrictions about working with controlled substances, there are very few volunteer opportunities available in a pharmacy setting.

Skills and Personality

Pharmacists must have strong analytical skills and be detail oriented. They are not only responsible for filling prescriptions accurately, they must also be able to draw on their extensive knowledge of drugs and their effects to be sure their patients do not suffer adverse reactions to the medications prescribed to them.

Pharmacists also advise their patients about how to take a medication and what side effects to watch out for. For this they need strong communication skills and should enjoy working with the public. While they are not always recognized as such, pharmacists are health care providers and are responsible for the well-being of their patients.

On the Job

Employers

Most pharmacists are employed by pharmacies and drugstores. About 10 percent of pharmacists are employed by hospitals or other health care facilities. Pharmacists can also own and operate their own pharmacies.

Working Conditions

Most pharmacists work in pharmacies, which may be located in drugstores, grocery stores, or health care facilities, including clinics and hospitals. Pharmacies can also be stand-alone establishments. Pharmacists involved in research work in laboratories, often in the research and development divisions of pharmaceutical companies. Pharmacists who teach work in an academic setting at a university or pharmacy school.

Most pharmacists work full time. Those who work in pharmacies that are open twenty-four hours may work nights or weekends. Pharmacists usually spend most of their workday standing, and sometimes they work long hours. "It's very common as a retail pharmacist to do 14-hour shifts without a break, without lunch, standing up for hours under fluorescent lights," one retail pharmacist explained to Alexa Tsoulis-Reay in an April 2017 article published on *New York* magazine's website. "I can't leave because, by law, the pharmacist has to be on-site, so if I left we'd have to shut down the whole shop." On the other hand, retail pharmacists can usually choose which shifts they work.

Earnings

The Bureau of Labor Statistics (BLS) reports that in 2016, the median salary for pharmacists was $122,230. The lowest-paid 10 percent of pharmacists earned less than $87,120, and the highest-paid 10 percent earned more than $157,950.

Pharmacists who work in a retail setting can often set their own shift schedule or pick up extra shifts, significantly increasing their income. Some retail pharmacies offer overtime pay to their pharmacists.

Opportunities for Advancement

Five to ten years into practice, most pharmacists have enough experience to advance in their careers. Pharmacists working in community pharmacies or hospitals move into managerial or supervisory positions and are eventually promoted to executive or leadership positions. Some experienced pharmacists are lured by high-paying jobs in the pharmaceutical industry, while others open their own stores or take teaching or research positions at universities.

What Is the Future Outlook for Pharmacists?

The outlook for pharmacists is uncertain. In 2015 *Forbes* magazine ranked pharmacist as the number one health care job in America due to a high starting salary and projected employment growth by the BLS of 14 percent through 2024. But by 2016 the BLS had revised its growth projection down to 3 percent through 2026. The problem, as pharmacist Jason Poquette sees it, is that pharmacy schools are graduating too many pharmacists. "More than half of the United States currently has a surplus of pharmacists, meaning the number of pharmacists looking for jobs outweighs the number of jobs available," he wrote in a March 2016 article in *Pharmacy Times*. He is concerned that this may eventually lead to lower wages and poorer working conditions for pharmacists. "It would be great if pharmacy schools would come together and mutually agree to reduce their enrollment, but that's unlikely," Poquette wrote.

This is not to say that the future is necessarily bleak for this profession. Pharmacists still command one of the highest starting salaries in the health care industry, and it is relatively easy to get a good job in a state that does not have a surplus of pharmacists. In addition, with the population aging, it is likely that the demand for pharmacists will increase dramatically in coming years. In fact, because of an overall shortage of health care professionals, the role of the traditional pharmacist is already expanding. For instance, some states have created a new kind of pharmacist license designation called an advanced practice pharmacist. These pharmacists are health care providers who collaborate with doctors. They evaluate patients and order tests that assess how well their medications are working, and they prescribe, adjust, or discontinue drug therapies as needed. California has started awarding advanced practice licenses to pharmacists who have completed a residency program and met other requirements. "Advanced practice pharmacists are leading the profession," said Mel Baron, a professor at the University of Southern California School of Pharmacy. In a March 2017 article on the school's website, he stated, "This is the future of pharmacy."

Find Out More

American Association of Colleges of Pharmacy (AACP)
1727 King St.
Alexandria, VA 22314
website: www.aacp.org

The AACP is a national organization that represents pharmacy education in the United States. Its website contains educational resources, a student center, and news and publications about pharmacy education.

American Pharmacists Association (APhA)
2215 Constitution Ave. NW
Washington, DC 20037
website: www.pharmacist.com

The APhA is the largest professional association of pharmacists in the United States. Its website contains a career pathways evaluation program that can help students interested in a career in pharmacy decide whether it is right for them. The website also contains hundreds of articles of interest to pharmacists, as well as access to the APhA magazine, *Student Pharmacist*.

American Society of Health-System Pharmacists (ASHP)
4500 East-West Hwy., Suite 900
Bethesda, MD 20814
website: www.ashp.org

The ASHP is a professional organization for pharmacists, student pharmacists, and pharmacy technicians. Its website has information for students and newly graduated pharmacists, articles about pharmacy practice, and current events and news articles about issues that impact pharmacy professionals.

Pharmacy Is Right for Me
website: http://pharmacyforme.org

Pharmacy Is Right for Me is a website devoted to helping students, parents, and educators learn about careers in the field of pharmacy. The website contains information about what it is like to be a pharmacist and how to become one, as well as opportunities for high school students to explore this career through internships and shadowing programs.

Phlebotomist

Derek Wilson's shift at the hospital begins hours before dawn. He is a phlebotomist, a medical technician trained in drawing blood. Because blood tests often require patients to be fasting and rested, he will need to draw blood from the majority of his patients before they eat their first meal of the day. He makes sure his cart is fully stocked with the equipment he will need and then prints out his orders. His first stop is the maternity ward, where he wakes several expectant mothers and asks them permission to draw their blood for testing. Next, he visits the intensive care unit, where many critically ill patients already have catheters inserted into their veins for blood draws. He returns to the laboratory, where he uses a device called a centrifuge to spin the vials of blood, separating the red blood cells from the plasma. He then arranges the vials to be transported to the various testing areas in the hospital and refills his phlebotomy cart. He will be called on throughout the day for special blood drawing requests, including prioritized blood draws from the emergency room. Finally, at the

At a Glance

Phlebotomist

Minimum Educational Requirements
Completion of phlebotomist training program

Personal Qualities
Strong people skills, accuracy, dexterity

Certification and Licensing
Required in almost all cases

Working Conditions
Indoors in hospital or laboratory settings

Salary Range
About $23,000 to $47,000

Number of Jobs
About 112,700

Future Job Outlook
Much faster than average

end of his workday, he visits the nursery, where he draws blood from the heels of newborns requiring testing.

A phlebotomist is considered an entry-level health care job, which means that it takes a year or less of training after high school. Phlebotomists are trained in venipuncture, or the puncturing of a vein with a hollow needle to collect blood. Many health care professionals, including nurses and doctors, draw blood, but while a nurse might draw blood several times in a day, a phlebotomist will draw blood dozens of times a day and is often more skilled at venipuncture than other health care professionals. Phlebotomists work mainly in hospitals, clinics, and blood donation centers. They interpret test orders, collect blood samples from patients, label vials of blood and prepare them for testing, and practice infection control.

Before phlebotomists can draw blood, they must assess their patients' draw sites. Most patients have blood drawn from a vein near the surface of the skin inside the elbow. However, in patients who have weak or thin veins or who are infants, it may be necessary to draw blood from another area. A phlebotomist can take blood from any vein that is close to the surface of the skin, such as the back of the hand, in the heel or the top of the foot, or even from the scalp. In addition, certain conditions, such as low blood pressure or dehydration, can make a blood draw difficult, and phlebotomists are trained to recognize these conditions and compensate for them. They must also be sure that their patients' medical conditions will not affect blood draw. For instance, people who are on blood-thinning medication can bleed profusely when their blood is taken, and the phlebotomist must be prepared to deal with this.

Taking someone's blood is no easy task. A phlebotomist must be prepared for a patient to become light-headed or even faint during a needle stick, in most cases due to a drop in blood pressure. This can be dangerous for both the patient and the phlebotomist, and is why blood banks or laboratories that draw blood have reclining chairs and offer their patients fruit juice or snacks after their blood is taken.

Unlike other types of medical and laboratory technicians, phlebotomists interact with patients all day long. To be successful as a phlebotomist, compassion is key. Many people are frightened of getting their blood drawn, and some even have a phobia, or irrational fear, of needles or blood. Therefore, an important part of a phlebotomist's job is to establish a trusting relationship with patients and to soothe their fears. "You have to respect their fear and explore its roots," explained Dennis Ernst, executive director of the Center for Phlebotomy Education. As he said in a February 2016 article by Amanda Koehler published on the Advance Healthcare Network's website, "Maybe the patient's first draw was at the hands of someone who wasn't properly trained, or just not trained to minimize the trauma of a venipuncture in the form of physical pain and mental anguish. Because you never know what kind of prior experience anxious patients might have had, you must be prepared to slow the process down and invest in a positive outcome."

Good phlebotomists, Ernst said, will acknowledge a patient's fears while reassuring them that they are in the hands of a trained professional. Sometimes explaining exactly what will happen can help allay a patient's fears; other times distraction or meditation techniques help. According to Ernst, phlebotomists who become impatient or are dismissive of their patients' fears should not work with anxious patients. "I hear too many stories about patients who were ridiculed and belittled for being nervous or afraid of needles," he told Koehler. "Those who realize they're not wired to draw from anxious patients should find someone else to perform the procedure. Otherwise, the patient's fears will be realized, and they could develop a lifelong aversion to healthcare."

Children present a special challenge to phlebotomists. Most children are frightened by needles, and many will squirm or struggle when their blood is drawn. When this happens, they are at great risk for injuring themselves, so usually another phlebotomist or health care professional will gently restrain children who need to have their blood drawn and distract them with a television program or picture book. Because children are notoriously difficult to keep calm during a blood draw, some phlebotomists specialize in pediatric care.

How Do You Become a Phlebotomist?

Education

Phlebotomy training programs require a high school diploma or equivalent. Typically, they take one year or less to complete and are available at community colleges, vocational schools, and technical schools. Students learn anatomy, physiology, and medical terminology. They also learn good lab practices.

Certification and Licensing

Almost all employers require that their phlebotomists be certified by a reputable professional agency. California, Louisiana, Nevada, and Washington all require phlebotomists to be certified in order to practice phlebotomy. Some employers will train phlebotomists on the job and allow them to delay certification.

Most certification programs require a student to have both classroom education and clinical experience. Certification exams usually include a written component and practical components, such as drawing blood.

Volunteer Work and Internships

There are few volunteer opportunities available in phlebotomy, but high school students may be able to secure a paid or unpaid internship in a health care laboratory. This will give them experience in good laboratory practices and allow them to watch phlebotomists at work.

Skills and Personality

One of the most important qualities of a phlebotomist is the ability to be accurate. Phlebotomists must interpret doctors' orders to the letter. They must also make sure that they do not mislabel blood samples or contaminate the samples in any way. Making a mistake can have dire consequences for a patient, who may be given the wrong treatment based on inaccurate test results. Phlebotomists must also follow sterilization procedures accurately and consistently to protect their own health and the health of their patients. People who are meticulous about accuracy make good phlebotomists.

Phlebotomists must also be good with their hands. Dexterity and good hand-eye coordination are crucial. Performing a successful and relatively pain-free blood draw takes manual dexterity and skill. Phlebotomists can greatly improve their skills through practice and experience.

Finally, because phlebotomists interact with the public, they must have excellent people skills. They must be professional, friendly, patient, and soothing. Phlebotomy is a great career for a person who likes both helping people and doing laboratory work.

On the Job

Employers

Most phlebotomists work in hospitals or medical and diagnostic laboratories. Some work for ambulatory health care services, which means that they travel to health care facilities or to people's homes to collect blood samples. A small percentage of phlebotomists work in doctors' offices.

Working Conditions

An important part of being a phlebotomist is understanding the danger posed by working with needles and being able to take preventive measures to avoid being stuck. A used needle is contaminated with a patient's blood. Many blood-borne diseases are extremely dangerous, and some cannot be cured. For this reason, phlebotomists take special precautions to avoid coming into contact with the blood of their patients. For instance, they are trained not to recap a needle once it is used to avoid a needle puncture, and they dispose of all used needles in special containers designed for sharp objects. They also wear gloves and other protective equipment. Even though precautions are taken, phlebotomists are more at risk for contracting a blood-borne disease than the general population.

Most phlebotomists work full time. Phlebotomists who work in laboratories or doctors' offices keep a regular work schedule, but those who work in hospitals may be required to work shifts that start very early in the morning. Since phlebotomists must be available at all hours of the day, they also work overnight shifts, weekends, and holidays.

Most hospital phlebotomists are required to walk from patient to patient and are on their feet for most of the day.

Earnings

According to the Bureau of Labor Statistics (BLS), in May 2016 the median salary for phlebotomists was $32,420. The lowest-paid 10 percent earned less than $23,330, and the highest-paid 10 percent earned more than $46,850. Phlebotomists who work in laboratories tend to earn slightly more than those who work in health care settings, such as hospitals or physicians' offices.

Opportunities for Advancement

Phlebotomists can advance in their field by moving into management or supervisory roles. They can increase their pay by switching employers as they gain experience. According to the Phlebotomy Training Group, reference laboratories (laboratories that do specialized testing for other laboratories) pay the most, offering a median wage of $20.16 an hour.

Another way to advance in this field is to specialize. Phlebotomists can earn several advanced certifications. One such certification is called a Donor Phlebotomy Technician (DPT). A DPT is authorized to work in blood-collection centers. After five years on the job, a DPT earns about $48,000 per year.

Many phlebotomists decide to advance their careers by becoming medical or laboratory technicians, which requires completing an associate's degree and attending an accredited training program. Other phlebotomists go into nursing, which also requires additional education and training. Because a phlebotomist's schedule is often flexible, many find that they can take classes while they work. Some hospitals even have tuition reimbursement programs for phlebotomists who want to advance their careers.

What Is the Future Outlook for Phlebotomists?

The BLS reports that employment for phlebotomists is projected to grow by 25 percent from 2014 to 2024, much faster than average. This is due in part to the overall projected increase in patient load due to population aging. In addition, there is high turnover in this profession, as many phlebotomists go on to train for other careers. Phlebotomists who are certified by reputable organizations such as the National Center for Competency Testing will have the best job prospects.

Find Out More

American Medical Technologists (AMT)
10700 W. Higgins Rd., Suite 150
Rosemont, IL 60018

The AMT is an internationally recognized certification agency and membership society for medical technicians and technologists, including phlebotomists. Its website contains information about phlebotomy training, how to become certified, and where to find a job as a phlebotomist.

Center for Phlebotomy Education
PO Box 5
2129 Edsel Lane
Corydon, IN 47112
website: www.phlebotomy.com

The Center for Phlebotomy Education is an advocacy association for phlebotomists in the United States. Its website contains information about the science of phlebotomy, how to find a reputable phlebotomy school, and phlebotomy certification organizations.

Phlebotomy Examiner
website: www.phlebotomyexaminer.com

Phlebotomy Examiner is a website devoted to helping students decide whether phlebotomy is a good career choice for them. It has dozens of articles related to what it is like to be a phlebotomist, as well as job and career advice for phlebotomists.

Phlebotomy Training Group
website: http://phlebotomytraininggroup.com

Phlebotomy Training Group is a website that contains comprehensive information about phlebotomy training and certification in the United States. It has detailed information about what it is like to be a phlebotomist, how to find training and certification programs, and how to get a job as a phlebotomist.

Obstetrician

By 7:15 a.m. Dr. Connie Faro, an obstetrician in Houston, Texas, is scrubbing up for a cesarean section, or C-section—a procedure in which a baby is delivered surgically through an incision in the mother's abdomen and uterus. This is not Faro's first C-section of the day—a few hours before, she was called to the hospital to perform an emergency C-section. It also will not be her last—her third surgery is scheduled for 9:30 that morning. The expectant mothers under Faro's care are awake during the procedure, so they get to see their baby moments after the baby is born. Faro loves her job. "To spend nine months with somebody and then hand them a life you just brought into the world for them, it completes the circle," she told Craig Melvin in a November 4, 2015, segment of the morning television show *Today*.

Obstetricians care for pregnant women and deliver babies. Obstetricians are also gynecologists—doctors who specialize in the diseases specific to females, especially those that affect the reproductive system. These two specialties are taught together and are known as

At a Glance

Obstetrician

Minimum Educational Requirements
Doctor of medicine degree, four-year residency

Personal Qualities
Excellent critical-thinking and interpersonal skills, compassion

Certification and Licensing
License required; certifications optional

Working Conditions
Clinical settings

Salary Range
About $95,000 to $366,000

Number of Jobs
About 19,800

Future Job Outlook
Job growth much faster than average

obstetrics and gynecology, or ob-gyn. About 90 percent of doctors who have studied ob-gyn treat both pregnant and nonpregnant women. However, doctors who choose to focus on caring for pregnant women exclusively are called obstetricians. Those who choose to treat only nonpregnant women are called gynecologists.

Delivering babies is just a small part of an obstetrician's day. They also monitor the health of a pregnant woman and her developing fetus (a medical term that refers to unborn offspring) through regular office visits, ultrasounds, and various other types of tests. They support women through the process of pregnancy, advising them about how to stay healthy and cope with discomfort, such as morning sickness or leg pain. They also treat conditions of pregnancy and care for both the mother and child for a short time after birth.

There is a great need for obstetricians who can treat women with high-risk pregnancies. One such obstetrician is Michael Wolfe, a maternal-fetal medicine specialist in Wichita, Kansas. Once a month Wolfe leaves his practice in Wichita and travels nearly 250 miles (402 km) to Lakin, Kansas, where he treats more than a dozen expectant mothers. According to Benjamin Anderson, chief executive officer of the Kearny County Hospital in Lakin, Wolfe's visits are the only access to maternal-fetal medical services his patients have. "I know of at least two women . . . whose lives were saved by a direct and timely intervention by Dr. Wolfe," Anderson said in an August 2016 post by Roz Hutchinson on a blog on the Via Christi Health website.

How Do You Become an Obstetrician?

Becoming an obstetrician takes at least twelve years of higher education and training after high school. To prepare for this career, students should focus on math and science classes in high school, especially biology and chemistry.

Many college students who want to be obstetricians choose a premedical, or premed, track—a series of courses that prepares students for medical school. Students do not have to be on the premed track to be accepted to medical school; however,

An obstetrician listens for the fetal heartbeat. In addition to delivering babies, obstetricians monitor the health of pregnant women and their fetuses and help with any problems or discomfort during pregnancy.

medical schools require that students have completed specific courses in math and science, and a premed track includes these courses. It also prepares students to take the Medical College Admission Test (MCAT), a standardized test that is required for admission to medical schools in the United States. Doing well on the MCAT, getting good grades, completing the required courses, and showing a commitment to medicine through outside activities all help a student's chances of being accepted to one of the 179 medical schools in the United States.

Medical school is a four-year graduate school that all US doctors must complete as part of their medical training. Typically, a student's first two years are spent in the classroom and the second two years in a hospital or other clinical setting. Students receive training in a variety of medical specialties during the second two years. They also begin applying for a residency program—a program of extended training in a medical specialty.

Residents in ob-gyn work for four years in a hospital or clinical setting under supervision. During this time, the resident learns increasingly difficult procedures and surgeries and is given more and more responsibility in treating patients. The patients who are seen in residency programs tend to be very challenging, in part because the best ob-gyn centers often have residency programs. Because learning surgery is part of an ob-gyn residency, and because ob-gyn patients tend to have after-hours emergencies and deliveries, an ob-gyn residency is one of the most difficult residencies in terms of workload. In fact, many residents work seventy to one hundred hours per week. Robert Petres, an ob-gyn who practices in Richmond, Virginia, reported in an interview that during one five-month period of his residency, he delivered six hundred babies.

After completing their residency, doctors can attend a specialty training program called a fellowship. Ob-gyns interested in obstetrics can do a fellowship in maternal-fetal medicine, which trains them in the care of high-risk pregnancies. Fellowships are also available in gynecological oncology (cancer of the female reproductive system), female pelvic medicine/reconstructive surgery, and reproductive endocrinology (female fertility).

Certification and Licensing

Even though students graduate from medical school with a medical doctor, or MD, degree, they cannot practice medicine until they are licensed. The licensing process for doctors is complex and varies from state to state, but all states require doctors to pass standardized written and oral exams. During medical school and ob-gyn residency, students take a three-part exam called the United States Medical Licensing Examination (USMLE). They take the first part of the USMLE at the end of their second year of medical school, the second part during their fourth year, and the third after their first year of residency. Once they have passed all three parts of the USMLE and have completed all requirements for their residency, they may apply for a medical license.

Ob-gyn residents are not eligible to take the ob-gyn board certification exam until they are licensed and have been practicing medicine for at least two years. Those who have completed a fellowship must also take both an oral and written certification examination.

Volunteer Work and Internships

High school students interested in becoming obstetricians can volunteer at a local hospital or clinic to get experience in the health care field. Young people can become certified nursing assistants at sixteen years old, which may qualify them for a volunteer or paid internship in a women's health clinic.

Skills and Personality

The most successful obstetricians are able to create trusting relationships with their patients. Pregnant women must feel comfortable to discuss issues that are extremely emotional, personal, and sometimes embarrassing. For this reason, obstetricians must be compassionate and have excellent listening skills. Students who are uncomfortable with discussions about private or sensitive bodily functions should not become obstetricians.

In addition, like all physicians, obstetricians must have excellent critical-thinking and problem-solving skills. Strong academic skills and a drive to succeed will help students complete the difficult educational requirements necessary to become obstetricians.

On the Job

Employers

Most obstetricians have a private practice or work within ob-gyn group practices. About 20 percent of ob-gyns work for hospitals or outpatient care centers. A small percentage of ob-gyns work for colleges, universities, professional schools, or medical and diagnostic laboratories.

Working Conditions

Obstetricians work in clinical settings. According to the American Medical Association, they work as many or more hours per week than any other medical specialty. One reason for this is that babies are born at all hours of the day. While some obstetricians take turns delivering babies or dealing with emergencies after hours (sharing these duties with other doctors in their practice), many do not—in part because their patients prefer to give birth while being attended by their own doctor.

In addition, much of the work of obstetricians happens after they see their patients. For instance, when ob-gyn Renee Darko sees her last patient of the day, it often feels as if her work is just beginning. She must catch up on patient notes, interpret lab results, call in prescription refills, and address the questions or concerns of patients who contacted the office while she was seeing others.

Earnings

PayScale, a website that analyzes salary data, reports that in 2017, the salary range for ob-gyns was $95,996 to $366,002. The Bureau of Labor Statistics (BLS) reports that in 2016, the mean annual salary for ob-gyns was $234,310. The top earners work in medical and diagnostic laboratories in managerial and research positions, but there are only about eighty such positions nationwide. Most top-earning obstetricians work in private practice. It is important to note that ob-gyns usually pay the highest rates in malpractice insurance of all physicians, because the risks of pregnancy are high and distraught parents often seek litigation for unfortunate experiences under an ob-gyn's care. According to the Massachusetts Medical Society, ob-gyns pay about 40 percent of their income in malpractice insurance.

Opportunities for Advancement

Obstetricians who want to increase their earnings often focus on building their practice, but those interested in advancing their careers and increasing their reputations within their field usually seek out a position in a teaching hospital that emphasizes research. These doctors have already completed a fellowship and usually do a combination of patient care and teaching while they pursue their research interests. For instance, during his work in the 1970s and 1980s at the Medical College of Virginia in Richmond, Petres became interested in the ways in which new ultrasound technology could be used in obstetrics. Petres was one of the first to use the technology to examine a fetus in the womb. "Before then, the only information we had about a fetus was the heartbeat," he explains. "Working with ultrasound set the stage for thinking about the fetus as a separate patient and treating them inside the uterus." One of Petres's accomplishments was identifying and curing a deadly condition in which babies are born unable to breathe because fluid has accumulated around their lungs. Petres and his colleagues were the first to successfully remove this fluid while the fetus was still in the uterus.

According to Petres, the most exciting work in obstetrics today is being done in partnership with geneticists. Researchers in this field are working to improve methods of identifying and treating genetic disorders before babies are born.

What Is the Future Outlook for Obstetricians?

The BLS projects that employment of all physicians and surgeons will grow by 14 percent from 2014 to 2024, much faster than average. There is also a shortage of ob-gyns in the United States. This is in part because there has been no increase in the graduation rates of new ob-gyns since 1980—even though the female population has increased by 26 percent. For this reason, new obstetricians will have no difficulty finding patients.

Being an obstetrician takes commitment and a willingness to work long hours. However, if those who are passionate about helping bring new life into the world can overcome these obstacles, they are guaranteed an exciting and fulfilling career.

Find Out More

American Congress of Obstetricians
and Gynecologists (ACOG)
409 Twelfth St. SW
Washington, DC 20024
website: www.acog.org

ACOG is a professional organization for ob-gyns dedicated to the improvement of women's health. Its website has a wealth of information about obstetrics and careers in obstetrics, as well as links to hundreds of publications for ob-gyns and students.

ObGyn.net
website: www.obgyn.net

ObGyn.net is a website that disseminates information, articles, news stories, and videos of interest to ob-gyns and students interested in this career. Registration is free and gives students access to all areas of the website.

Obgynstudent.com
website: www.obgynstudent.com

Obgynstudent.com is a resource for medical students specializing in ob-gyn. The website contains articles, presentations, and videos that will give readers considering a career in the field information about ob-gyn education and practice.

Student Doctor Network
website: www.studentdoctor.net

The Student Doctor Network is a resource for students and doctors. The website has articles about what medical school is like and what different types of doctors—including ob-gyns—do in practice, resources for people considering a career in medicine, and a quiz that helps students identify the best medical specialty for them.

Interview with a Psychologist

Margaret Duvall is a clinical psychologist with more than thirty years of experience. She practices in Richmond, Virginia, where she specializes in adult psychotherapy and couples counseling. Duvall spoke to the author about her career.

Q: Why did you become a psychologist?

A: I used to teach social studies to middle school students, which I enjoyed, but I was not good at teaching historical dates or battles. Instead I liked to figure out what the people in that period of history were thinking. When I was renewing my teaching license I took a continuing education course in psychology. My professor was running a study on a psychiatric ward about people who compulsively ate paper. I collected data about their thoughts. Afterward, the professor took me aside and said I might make a good clinician! That was a turning point in my life—for someone to tell me I had skills to be a clinical psychologist was very exciting, and I realized that's what I really wanted to do.

Q: Can you describe your typical workday?

A: I'm a solo practitioner, and I do my own paperwork, so three days a week I come in and set up the office and then see patients. Therapy is a process, and its course is different for everyone. In the first visit, I learn from them about their current life problems, and we both decide whether we are a good fit to work together. In the second, I ask them to tell me their life story. As I get to know them, I look into my "toolbox" to see what therapeutic techniques might be useful. Some patients benefit from hypnosis, others from behavioral therapy, and sometimes psychoanalytical tools are useful.

One thing I ask my patients is to not censor themselves in the session. I want them to say whatever comes to mind. Then I ask them to imagine they are placing what they have said on a table between us, so we can both look at it together and try to figure out what it means. This process is often difficult and uncomfortable, and it gets better after the patient has seen that I can be trusted with whatever comes to their mind. Therapy works by really establishing a healthy relationship in the sessions.

Q: What do you like most about your job?
A: The most enjoyable part of my job is when one of my patients tells me that something we did in our sessions helped them. I won't know for sure what element of therapy will be helpful, so for me, hearing about what worked for them out in their lives outside the therapy is the big payoff.

Q: What do you like least about your job?
A: The least enjoyable part of my job is managing all of the legal and ethical rules that we psychologists follow. It can be complex to protect confidentiality, and it's really important to do that, even when it's hard.

Q: What personal qualities do you find most valuable for this type of work?
A: Curiosity. The best therapists are seriously curious about how other people think. I am fascinated by people in general—regardless of the issues they face—and I'm especially interested in working with them when I sense a connection between us.

An effective therapist is willing to learn how to listen. Listening well is not easy, and it does not come naturally. It is a skill that we develop and practice.

Q: What is the best way to prepare for this type of job?
A: Take part in group therapy in an area that interests you. Check with your local hospital or community health center to see whether there are any groups for teens. You can benefit from getting the perspective of a good therapist, and joining a therapy group will

give you an idea of what therapy is and how it works. It will also give you the patient's perspective, which will help you enormously if you pursue a career in psychology.

Also, if you can, attend a psychology meeting or lecture on a subject that interests you. Some psychology conferences allow the public to attend their lectures, and psychologists sometimes give public talks at local colleges, churches, or community centers.

Q: What other advice do you have for students who might be interested in this career?
A: Make sure you want to be a psychologist for the right reasons. I've noticed that some people who say they are interested in psychology actually just like to diagnose the people they meet. And they always seem to diagnose them with the very worst disorders! But being a good clinician is not about labeling people; it's about really listening to another person and helping them understand themselves. That's where the real satisfaction from this job comes from.

Other Jobs in Health Care

Ambulance driver
Cardiovascular technologist
Chiropractor
Clinical laboratory
    technician
Dental assistant
Dentist
Diagnostic medical
    sonographer
Gastroenterologist
Genetic counselor
Hearing aid specialist
Home health aide
Magnetic resonance imaging
    technologist
Massage therapist

Medical coder
Medical records technician
Medical secretary
Medical transcriptionist
Nutritionist
Occupational therapist
Ophthalmologist
Optician
Pediatrician
Pharmacy technician
Physical therapist
Physician assistant
Radiologist
Respiratory therapist
Speech-language pathologist
Surgeon

Editor's note: The US Department of Labor's Bureau of Labor Statistics provides information about hundreds of occupations. The agency's *Occupational Outlook Handbook* describes what these jobs entail, the work environment, education and skill requirements, pay, future outlook, and more. The *Occupational Outlook Handbook* may be accessed online at www.bls.gov/ooh.

Index

Note: Boldface page numbers indicate illustrations.